Adventures Of A

Product Launch Chaos

Turning Product Launch Mistakes Into Digital Business Product Launch Success

By

Dr Ope Banwo

Author Of Confessions Of a Guru-Wannabe

Copyright Page

Copyright © 2024 Ope Banwo

All rights reserved. No part of this book may be reproduced, distributed, or transmitted in any form or by any means, including photocopying, recording, or other electronic or mechanical methods, without the prior written permission of the publisher, except in the case of brief quotations embodied in critical reviews and certain other noncommercial uses permitted by copyright law.

For permission requests, write to the publisher at the address below:

Netpreneur Books, 3568 Dodge Streeet. Omaha, NE 68131

Ceo@Netpreneur360.com

This book is a work of fiction. Names, characters, places, and incidents are either the product of the author's imagination or used fictitiously. Any resemblance to actual events, locales, or persons, living or dead, is entirely coincidental.

Table of Contents

Adventures Of A Guru Wannabe:**Product Launch Chaos**

Turning Product Launch Mistakes Into Digital Business Product Launch Success By Dr Ope Banwo

Copyright Page

About the Author

Why I Wrote This Book

Prologue: The High Stakes of Launching Online Products

Chapter 1: The Illusion of Perfection

Chapter 2: Dreaming Big, Falling Hard

Chapter 3: The Lone Recruiter

Chapter 4: The Missing Hype

Chapter 5: The One-Shot Wonder

Chapter 6: Overreliance on a Single Platform

Chapter 7: The Last-Minute Panic

Chapter 8: The Unforeseen Troubles

Chapter 9: The Unmotivated Partners

Chapter 10: Out of Sight, Out of Mind

Chapter 11: The Stingy Sponsor

Chapter 12: The Lost Traffic

Chapter 13: The Deflated Dream

Chapter 14: Ignoring the Lessons

Chapter 15: The Halfway Halt

Chapter 16: Quality Over Quantity

Chapter 17: The Silent Channel

Chapter 18: The Unforeseen Troubles

Chapter 19: Unwillingness to Reward Partners

Chapter 20: The Blind Eye to Competition

Chapter 21: Neglecting Customer Feedback

Chapter 22: Overestimating the Market

Chapter 23: Inadequate Support System

Chapter 24: The Overlooked Analytics

Epilogue: The Journey Continues

About the Author

Dr. Ope Banwo is a seasoned digital marketer, entrepreneur, and author with a passion for helping others succeed in the digital marketing space. With over a decade of experience in creating, launching, and marketing digital products, Dr. Banwo has built a reputation for his innovative strategies and dedication to excellence.

Dr. Banwo is the founder of several successful online businesses and has coached countless entrepreneurs on how to achieve their goals through effective digital marketing practices. His expertise spans various areas, including content creation, social media marketing, email marketing, and product launches.

In addition to his entrepreneurial ventures, Dr. Banwo is a sought-after speaker and trainer, sharing his insights and knowledge at conferences and workshops around the world. His commitment to continuous learning and improvement has made him a trusted authority in the digital marketing community.

Through his writing, Dr. Banwo aims to inspire and empower aspiring marketers and entrepreneurs, offering practical advice and sharing his own experiences to help them navigate the complexities of the digital world. His latest book, "Adventures of a Guru-Wannabe: The Product Launch Saga," is a testament to his journey and the lessons he has learned along the way.

Dr. Banwo holds a Ph.D. in Business Administration and is an advocate for leveraging technology to create opportunities and drive success. When he's not working on his next project, he enjoys spending time with his family, traveling, and exploring new cultures.

For more information, visit www.FearlessNetpreneur.com[1] or follow Dr. Ope Banwo on social media:

- Facebook: www.facebook.com/opebanwopage
- Twitter: www.twitter.com/opebanwo
- Instagram: www.Instagram.com/opebanwo
- LinkedIn: www.Linkedin.com/in/opebanwo

---

1. http://www.FearlessNetpreneur.com

Why I Wrote This Book

When I first embarked on my journey as a digital marketer, I was filled with excitement, ambition, and a vision of success. However, I quickly realized that the path to achieving my goals was fraught with challenges, mistakes, and unexpected setbacks. Each step of the journey taught me invaluable lessons, shaping my understanding of what it takes to succeed in the ever-evolving world of digital marketing.

"Adventures of a Guru-Wannabe: The Product Launch Saga" is a reflection of my experiences, struggles, and triumphs. I wrote this book to share the lessons I've learned, hoping to provide guidance and inspiration to other aspiring digital marketers. This book is not just a collection of success stories; it is an honest account of the mistakes I made and the valuable insights I gained along the way.

Throughout my journey, I encountered numerous challenges, from technical glitches and unmotivated affiliates to market misjudgments and inadequate support systems. Each of these experiences taught me something new and reinforced the importance of resilience, adaptability, and continuous learning. By sharing these stories, I aim to help others navigate their own paths with greater confidence and insight.

I also wanted to emphasize the importance of perseverance. Success is not about avoiding mistakes but about learning from them and pushing forward despite the obstacles. I hope that by reading this book, you will find the motivation to keep pursuing your dreams, knowing that every challenge is an opportunity for growth.

Thank you for joining me on this journey. I am excited to see where your path takes you and hope that the insights and lessons shared in this book will help you achieve your goals.

Best, Opsy Bee

Prologue: The High Stakes of Launching Online Products

Opsy Bee leaned back in his chair, staring at the vision board on the wall of his home office. Pictures of successful product launches, motivational quotes, and his own scribbled notes covered the board. It was his constant reminder of where he wanted to be—a successful digital marketer with a series of hit product launches under his belt. But the road to success was fraught with challenges, and Opsy was about to embark on one of his most ambitious projects yet.

The idea had been brewing for months. Opsy knew that a successful product launch could catapult his business to new heights. He had studied the greats, attended countless webinars, and devoured every piece of content he could find on the subject. But there was a world of difference between theory and practice, and Opsy was about to find out just how steep that learning curve could be.

As he gathered his thoughts and prepared for the journey ahead, Opsy couldn't help but feel a mix of excitement and trepidation. The stakes were high. A successful launch could mean financial freedom, recognition, and the ability to make a real impact in the lives of his audience. But failure... failure was a constant shadow, lurking just out of sight.

Determined to face the challenge head-on, Opsy set out to plan his product launch. He knew he would need to be meticulous, strategic, and above all, resilient. The path ahead was uncertain, but Opsy was ready to navigate the labyrinth of product launches, armed with his passion, knowledge, and the hard-earned lessons from his previous ventures.

This is the story of Opsy Bee's journey through the trials and tribulations of launching a digital product. It's a tale of perseverance, mistakes, and invaluable lessons. Join Opsy as he navigates the complexities of the product launch world, learns from his missteps, and strives to turn his vision into reality.

Welcome to the Product Launch Saga.

Chapter 1: The Illusion of Perfection

The Fantasy of Perfection

Opsy Bee has no trouble with ambition. He felt urgent as he sat at his messy desk. His most ambitious endeavor thus was a thorough digital marketing course. He imagined a big launch with hundreds of excited clients waiting to buy his course. Opsy made a crucial error, though, in his enthusiasm—he undervalued the time and effort needed for such an undertaking.

Opsy chose to call his friend and mentor, Maria, on a clear morning. "Maria, I'm ready to start my new course," he exclaimed with much energy. Having worked on it for weeks, I believe it to be ideal. I want to get it out right away.

Maria answered gently. "Opsy, you seem eager, but have you given careful thought to completely organize everything? A major launch calls for more than just a fantastic offering. You have to arrange your sales funnel, create your marketing plan, and make sure everything is ready far in advance.

Opsy dismiss her worries. All of it is under control. I built the sales page, recorded the videos, and even penned the material. How hard can it be?

Maria exhaled. "Opsy, introducing a product goes beyond only its actual nature. It's about the whole process—exciting your audience, interacting with them, and making sure the launch day runs perfectly. Trust me; spend some time carefully organizing things.

Driven to prove her incorrect, Opsy threw herself into his launch planning. Often late into the night, he labored nonstop to perfect every element. But holes started to show as the launch date drew near. He knew he hadn't given enough time for funnel testing since the sales

PRODUCT LAUNCH CHAOS

page wasn't converting as effectively as he'd intended. His pre-launch material felt hurried and unpolished, and the affiliate recruiting process was rushed.

Opsy sensed the strain building on the eve of the launch. For a second view, he phoned another mentor, Jay. "Jay, I feel like I'm missing something even though I'm about to start my course. Regarding what should I do?

Jay spoke in a cool, soothing manner. Opsy, you seem to have jumped right into this. A good launch calls for thorough preparation and organization. You have to back off to make sure you have addressed all your bases. You should have tested your sales funnel. You have interacted with your audience? Is your marketing plan strong?

Opsy sighed, understanding the weight of his supervising. "I have some of it, but not as completely as I ought to have. Simply said, I wanted everything to be flawless.

Jay gave a subdued chuckle. "Opsy, perfect is a delusion. Emphasize on making things right, not perfect. Step back, postpone the launch if necessary, and check everything is in order. Delayed launch is preferable than an unsuccessful one.

Opsy chose to postpone the release with heavy heart. Through a sequence of pre-launch emails and materials, he spent extra time carefully testing his sales funnel, honing his marketing plan, and interacting with his audience. He guaranteed his associates were motivated and well-prepared and hired more associates.

Opsy was nervous and excited at the same time when the amended launch date finally showed up. Now it was time to see the outcomes; he had done all he could to get ready. Opsy came to see the value of careful preparation and planning as the sales began to flow and nice client comments arrived in.

When he thought back on the trip, Opsy realized his launch had almost been disrupted by the idea of perfection. Through meticulous preparation and planning, he had turned a possible tragedy into a triumphant product introduction. It was a priceless lesson that will direct him on his next projects.

Opsy knew this was only the start as he celebrated his accomplishment with Maria and Jay. The story of the product release was far from finished, and he was ready for whatever obstacles stood ahead.

Chapter 2: Dreaming Big, Falling Hard

Opsy Bee was riding high on the success of his well thought out release. Confident once more, he focused on his next target—a six-figure product release. He imagined a great show that would position him as a big participant in the realm of digital marketing. Stories of overnight triumphs and mega-launches drove Opsy's aspirations upward. But as he would soon discover, ambition devoid of foundation in reality can cause a nasty trip.

The ambitious course on advanced social media strategy included special tools and materials. Opsy felt that would be his pass to the major leagues. Driven to pay off his efforts, he gave the course material his whole heart and soul.

Opsy contacted Jay one evening to reveal his brilliant idea. "Jay, this is it." My intended launch is six figures. I know I can too, having watched others achieve it.

Jay answered softly, wary. "Opsy, aiming high is fantastic, but keep in mind that those six-figure launches you have heard about do not happen over night. Often the outcome of years of networking, relationship development, and market knowledge is their result. Have you thought about what it actually takes to execute such a major launch?

Ozzy dismissed Jay's worries. "After some investigation, I have I am doing what I know. I have a strong product and have scheduled some affiliates. It's going to be really large.

Jay warned, but Opsy persisted, creating a strict schedule and funding marketing and advertising aggressively. Driven by the buzz he was creating, he imagined legions of people flocking to purchase his course. But reality started to seep in as the launch date became near.

The lukewarm response from his associates was the first hint of trouble. Many of them were dedicated to other projects and lacked the attention his launch required. Opsy had lacked the significant promotional backing he had expected from his very last-minute outreach activities.

Opsy watched nervously on launch day as the sales figures dropped in. The answer fell much short of his expectations. The outcomes were depressing, notwithstanding the money spent on advertising and the attempts to generate awareness. Opsy had aimed for the heavens, but his rocket fell short.

Depressed, Opsy turned to Maria for guidance. Maria, I find unclear. I behaved exactly. Why didn't it go as planned?

Maria spoke softly yet with firmness. "Opsy, you had unrealistically high expectations but great ambition." Six-figure launches result from much more than just a fantastic product and effective marketing. They call for close ties to associates, a strong reputation, and occasionally even a little of luck. Although your aspirations are commendable, you should balance them with reality.

Driven to grow from his past, Opsy chose to stand back and rethink his strategy. Success, he realized, was about meticulous planning, reasonable goals, and laying a strong basis rather than only about great dreams.

Opsy buried himself in studying from other great marketers over the next three weeks. He examined their approaches, schedules, and techniques for developing close ties among associates. Eager to know where he had gone wrong and how he may grow, he asked peers and mentors for comments.

Opsy's efforts paid off over time. He came to see that creating a successful product launch required establishing the foundation for long-term success rather than pursuing short successes. He began to give networking, building rapport with associates, and creating reasonable goals more top priority.

Opsy discovered fresh direction as he got ready for his next launch. Though he understood the value of dreaming large, he also knew of the need of staying anchored in reality. He was laying himself for long-term success by combining ambition with sensible expectations and thorough preparation.

When he thought back on his path, Opsy realized how crucial it was to grow from every event—including both achievements and setbacks. Though it was still alive, the dream of a six-figure launch was now restrained with prudence and pragmatism.

With the knowledge he had gained and the will to keep on, Opsy Bee was ready for the next chapter—the product launch tale was far from finished.

Chapter 3: The Lone Recruiter

Opsy Bee was resolved to make his next product launch successful, firmly in mind the lessons from his last one. He had come to see the value of reasonable expectations and careful preparation. Now he was ready. Alternatively he thought. One vital component still escaped him: good affiliate recruiting.

Opsy understood that his launch can be ruined or enhanced depending on his network of affiliates. Reaching a larger audience and producing the excitement required for a good launch depend on affiliates. But his past efforts to assemble associates had been hurried and last-minute, therefore lacking the support he need. Driven not to make the same error, Opsy started his affiliate recruitment process early on.

Opsy made the decision one afternoon to call Maria for guidance on creating a strong affiliated network. "Maria, I have to get early this time affiliates on board. How best to contact them to make sure they are enthusiastic in advertising my product?

Maria responded pragmatically and wisely. "Opsy, relationships are the secret. First, find possible associates that fit your product and personally contact them. Show them the advantages of advertising your product, give them a preview of it, and make sure they feel appreciated. It's about your actions for them as much as about what they can do for you.

Following Maria's counsel, Opsy compiled a list of possible partners—people and companies with the attention and clout to have a big impact. He created tailored emails stressing the special worth of his offering and the advantages of affiliating oneself. To reward them, he also provided special bonuses and higher commission rates.

PRODUCT LAUNCH CHAOS

Opsy emailed and watched nervously for replies. Days went by with no response at all, and Opsy started to worry. Had he started once more late? Was his offer not appealing enough?

Under pressed, Opsy decided to ask Jay for further direction. "Jay, I find it difficult to get associates on board. I have emailed people, but the answers have been disappointing. What action ought I to take?

Jay responded with encouragement. "Opsy, developing an affiliate network calls for patience and effort. Follow up with anyone you spoke with, but avoid being overly demanding. Show real interest in their job and figure out how you may help them too. Go to networking gatherings, interact on social media, and exercise patience. Relationships cannot be created over night.

Jay's counsel energized Opsy, which boosted his efforts. He participated in online forums, went to virtual networking events, and connected with possible associates on social media. Following up on his first emails, he sent tailored messages asking to work on guest blog entries and webinar presentations.

The answers began to flow slowly but definitely. One email especially noteworthy from a well-known digital marketer called Lisa caught my attention.

"Hey Opsy,

Appreciate you getting in touch. I value your customized message and the thorough material on your goods. Learning more and looking at how we may cooperate interests me. Allow us to arrange a call to go over further.

Better still, Lisa Opsy was bursting with enthusiasm. Driven to provide a strong impression, he booked a call with Lisa and got ready completely.

Impressed with Opsy's passion and quality of his goods, Lisa agreed to become an affiliate and the call went well.

Inspired by this achievement, Opsy kept expanding his affiliated network. He developed partnerships, gave insightful material, and sent frequent updates on the evolution of the product line. His tenacity paid off; by the time the launch date drew near, he had a strong network of eager friends ready to advertise his offering.

The help of his associates clearly changed things on launch day. Sales began to flow consistently, and the buzz his associates produced set off a chain reaction. Opsy's early recruiting initiatives and meticulous planning were at last paying off.

When she thought back on the experience, Opsy saw how crucial it was to begin affiliate hiring early and foster meaningful relationships. The success of his release was evidence of the need of tenacity and the power of a solid network.

Ozzy knew the road was far from finished as he rejoiced with Maria and Jay. The story of the product launch included fresh lessons and difficulties every chapter. Equipped with the information and expertise from his most recent launch, Opsy was prepared to face whatever was ahead.

Chapter 4: The Missing Hype

The most recent release by Opsy Bee had given him insightful knowledge about affiliate recruitment and planning. He grew more assured as he got ready for his next product release. He had a well-considered strategy, a good network of associates, and a quality product. One key component, though, he still had to learn: creating pre-launch buzz.

Opsy had always thought that a great product would speak for itself, but he quickly came to see that generating hype before the release was as crucial. Even the best items could fall short without expectation and enthusiasm.

Opsy resolved to stay clear of this trap and contacted Maria for guidance on creating a successful pre-launch plan. "Maria, I'm nervous about creating enough hype even though I have everything set for the debut. How can I get everyone buzzing before the release?

Maria answered with great passion. "Opsy, a pre-launch plan that works well is all about inspiring your audience and creating buzz. People must be excited and curious enough to want to see what you have to offer. To keep your viewers interested, use teaser material, behind-the-scenes peeks, and exclusive previews.

Maria's advise was taken to heart, and Opsy started generating ideas for creating buzz. He made the decision to produce a run of teaser videos, each providing a quick look at many facets of the product. In addition, he intended a behind-the-scenes blog series that would chronicle the process of creating the product and honor the diligence and effort involved.

Opsy began his career by creating brief, interesting films highlighting the special qualities and advantages of his product without revealing too much. Using appealing headlines and clever subtitles to draw viewers in, he posted these movies on his social media platforms. On his website, he also created a dedicated pre-launch page urging guests to register for special updates and early access.

Opsy penned a series of blog entries exploring the development process, the difficulties he encountered, and the discoveries he made to go alongside the videos. He made the material relevant and interesting by including personal stories and observations. Every blog article concluded with a call to action urging visitors to add themselves to his email list for extra exclusive content.

Opsy observed his audience growing more excited as the pre-launch campaign gathered steam. His email list started to expand and comments and shares on his social media posts climbed. Opsy felt a flash of confidence as the buzz grew.

He understood, though, that creating buzz was only one component of the equation. He had to design engaging and participative events if he was going to really captiv his audience. Opsy made the decision to schedule a series of live Q&A events whereby he would respond to inquiries, provide analysis, and offer first-hand product previews. He pushed these meetings especially, urging his listeners to take part and share the word about them.

The reply was quite strong. The live Q&A sessions drew a sizable audience and had great participation. Opsy's audience responded well to his genuineness and openness to provide behind-the-scenes information, therefore strengthening their bond and raising excitement around the release.

One particularly noteworthy email came from Emma, a subscriber. Hello Opsy,

PRODUCT LAUNCH CHAOS

I appreciate the great pre-launch materials! The live events, blog entries, and videos have been quite interesting. The finished work will be much awaited. Maintain your excellent effort.

best, Emma

Opsy experienced great gratification. Responding fast, he thanked Emma for her support and advised her to keep tuned for the launch.

Opsy kept gathering momentum as the launch date neared. He shared fresh teaser material and launch reminders in regular updates to his email list. To add even more excitement, he worked with his associates to produce joint campaigns and unique deals.

When the launch day eventually arrived, there was obvious enthusiasm. The pre-launch buzz had paid off; sales began to flow from the moment the product went live. Opsy's meticulous preparation and captivating pre-launch plan had generated a wave of expectation that drove the launch toward success.

When she thought back on the encounter, Opsy understood how crucial it was to generate buzz and interact with his audience prior to a release. He had guaranteed a great beginning for his product by building expectation and thrillfulness.

Ozzy knew the road was far from finished as he rejoiced with Maria and Jay. The story of the product launch carried fresh difficulties and insights in every chapter. Equipped with the wisdom and experience from his most recent launch, Opsy was prepared to face whatever was ahead.

Chapter 5: The One-Shot Wonder

Opsy Bee felt more confident knowing his pre-launch hype campaign was successful. He now understood the need of involving his audience and building suspense. But he started to see a concerning trend as he savored the triumph of his most recent release. Though sales first surged, enthusiasm in his product rapidly faded. He came to see that depending just on one product introduction was unsustainable. He had to see beyond the first sale if he was to create a profitable company.

Opsy was aware he had to take care of backend offerings. A solid backend plan would not only boost his income but also give his clients more value, thereby keeping them happy and involved. Driven to perfect this facet of his company, Opsy contacted Jay for guidance.

"Jay, I've been considering my next product introductions. They begin strong, but curiosity wanes rapidly. I have to figure out how to keep my clients involved and provide continuous income. What advice do you have?

Jay answered with a direct approach. "Opsy, you have to consider the whole client process." It transcends the first sale. You should have appropriate downsell and upsell offerings to go with your main product. Consider what extra value you might offer and how you might keep your clients returning for more.

Opsy started generating ideas for backend offers after he listened to Jay. He made the decision to develop a line of supplemental goods and services meant to improve the value of his primary business. These comprised personalized coaching sessions, advanced training courses, and special membership access.

Opsy created first advanced training courses delving further into the subjects of his primary course. These courses provided specific knowledge and practical ideas to enable his clients to reach even more success. He set reasonable prices for them, which attracted clients eager to keep their learning path open.

Opsy then developed bespoke coaching packages. Many of his clients would gain from one-on-one direction and encouragement, he realized. To enable clients to use what they had discovered, the coaching packages comprised individualized comments, customized plans, and continuous assistance. This gave Opsy more personal touch and let him establish closer bonds with his clients.

At last Opsy started a special membership program. The program provides access to a private community, monthly live Q&A sessions, and exclusive materials not found elsewhere. For his most devoted clients, this gave constant value and a sense of belonging.

Opsy created an automated email sequence introducing these offers at key moments to guarantee his backend offers were smoothly included into the client journey. Following a major product purchase, a buyer would get follow-up emails stressing the advantages of the advanced modules, coaching programs, and membership program. Every email was painstakingly written to highlight the extra value the client will get and meet their needs.

Opsy started to see good outcomes as the new backend approach was implemented. Main product buyers were now making investments in the advanced courses, registering for coaching sessions, and enrolling in the membership program. Apart from increasing Opsy's income, the extra sources enabled him to design a more environmentally friendly company model.

Opsy once got an email from a customer called Tom. Hello Oggy,

I wanted to say thank you for the fantastic assistance and material. The advanced courses have been really beneficial, and the coaching sessions have given me the confidence and clarity I required to push my company forward. The best choice I have made was joining the membership program. Maintaining your excellent work is fantastic.

Best, Tom said.

Opsy experienced a great degree of gratification. He answered fast, thanks Tom for his comments and expressing thanks for the support.

When Opsy thought back on the road, she saw how crucial a solid rear is. He had established a more successful and environmentally friendly company by considering beyond the original sale and offering continuous value. The encounter had shown him that developing long-term bonds with his clients and always satisfying their needs were the paths to actual success.

Opsy understood the trip was far from finished as he celebrated with Maria and Jay. The story of the product introduction carried fresh difficulties and insights in every chapter. Equipped with the information and expertise from his most recent launch, Opsy was prepared to face whatever was ahead.

Chapter 6: Too much reliance on one platform

The success of his fresh backend approach delighted Opsy Bee. His items were selling well, and his clients were more involved than they had been. But he understood he couldn't rely on one platform for his launches if he was to have long-term success. He had mostly used Warrior Special Offers (WSO) for his product introductions up until now, and although it had been a strong basis, Opsy knew it was time to vary.

Opsy made the decision to call Maria one evening seeking guidance on increasing his influence. Maria, I have been considering. WSOs had some success for me, however depending too much on one platform seems like limiting me. What then ought I to do?

Maria answered with some encouragement. "Opsy, you are totally correct. Although WSOs are a fantastic starting point, the internet marketing scene is somewhat large. To get a larger audience, you must investigate other platforms and channels. Have you thought about using ClickBank, JVZoo, or maybe organizing your own launches?

Opsy nodded quietly. Although I have heard of them, I have not particularly investigated them. How best do you suppose one may get started?

Maria gave some sensible advise. "Start by looking at every platform. Examine the products that sell successfully, the audience makeup, and the commission systems. After your research, decide on one or two platforms to test your upcoming launch. You might even think about creating your own email list and straight traffic driving to your sales pages.

Opsy started looking at other sites, resolved to vary his approach. ClickBank and JVZoo caught his attention especially since they provided strong affiliate networks and a wide audience. Drawn by ClickBank's reputation and the possibility to reach a fresh audience, he chose to begin his next release with that company.

Setting up his goods on ClickBank, Opsy carefully created the sales page to appeal to this new market. Examining successful launches on the platform, he noted the tactics that succeeded and the typical mistakes to steer clear. He started creating his own email list as well, drawing members using lead magnets and focused advertising.

Opsy was excited and nervous at the same time as the launch date became close. Though it was a risk, he was ready to venture outside his comfort zone and investigate other venues. Now it was time to see the outcomes; he had worked for this.

Opsy observed on launch day as the sales began to trickle in. ClickBank received a positive response; new clients found his product and associates enthusiastically pushed it. The variety of the platform attracted a range of clients, therefore broadening Opsy's influence beyond what WSOs alone had accomplished.

One email particularly noteworthy from a new client called Sarah caught my attention. "Hi Opsy,"

I simply wanted to say thank you for the excellent material after seeing your product on ClickBank. After considerable searching for something like this, your course was above my expectations. Maintain the excellent effort!

Best, Sarah Opsy was pleased with herself. He answered fast, thanks Sarah for her support and advised her to keep in touch for next updates.

When he thought back on the experience, Opsy saw how crucial it was to vary his launch sites. He had attracted more people and raised more money by looking outside WSOs and investigating ClickBank. The success of this release confirmed the need of not depending only on one basket.

Ozzy knew the road was far from finished as he rejoiced with Maria and Jay. The story of the product introduction carried fresh difficulties and insights in every chapter. Equipped with the wisdom from his most recent launch, Opsy was prepared to face whatever happened next.

Chapter 7: The Last-Minute Panic

Opsy Bee had made a wise choice in diversifying his launch platforms. With a fresh sense of achievement, he was excited to use the knowledge he had gained for the launch of his next product. But there was one lesson he still didn't entirely get: the value of extensive testing. Opsy was under pressure to complete his next launch on time and was tempted to skimp on testing, a choice that would come back to haunt him.

Opsy was confident because the product was ready and the marketing strategy was in place. In an attempt to reach yet another new audience, he had selected JVZoo for this launch. But with only a few days remaining before the launch, Opsy discovered he had overlooked one essential step: a comprehensive testing of the sales funnel.

Jay had left Opsy a message, and her phone buzzed. "Opsy, how are things progressing with the launch? Has the sales funnel been tested?

Opsy had a twinge of regret. "Hey Jay, I haven't had time to test the funnel as completely as I should have because I've been so busy with the content and marketing. But it should be alright, in my opinion.

Jay gave a prompt and decisive response. "Opsy, you must test every possibility." Don't think it will function. Issues at the last minute can ruin your launch completely. Now is the time to make sure everything is operating as it should.

Opsy felt the weight of the approaching deadline, even though he knew Jay was correct. To make sure, he chose to test the sales funnel a couple times quickly. He proceeded with the launch since everything appeared to be going according to plan.

On the day of launch, Opsy felt anxious. Sales began to come in after a promising initial response. But then something terrible happened. After

PRODUCT LAUNCH CHAOS

making a purchase, some customers were unable to access their product, and others were having problems with the payment process. As Opsy frantically tried to pinpoint and resolve the issues, panic broke out.

Frantically, Opsy called Maria. "I'm having a bad dream, Maria." Customers are unable to access the goods due to glitches in the payment procedure. How should I proceed?

Maria gave a cool, encouraging remark. "Opsy, inhale deeply. Engage in conversation with your clients first. Inform them that you are aware of the problem and are attempting to fix it. Proceed with troubleshooting next. Determine the issue, and don't be afraid to ask for assistance from your tech support or the community.

Following Maria's advice, Opsy promptly acknowledged the problem and assured his clients that it would be fixed shortly in an email. He then jumped into troubleshooting mode, asking his tech support team for assistance in locating and resolving the issue.

After several hours, the problems were fixed, allowing users to use the goods at last. In a follow-up email, Opsy expressed regret for the trouble and offered a bonus as a token of appreciation for their endurance. His clients responded with understanding, and many expressed gratitude for his openness and sincere attempts to put things right.

Mike, a customer, sent me one really noteworthy email. Hello Opsy

I appreciate your timely updates and your swift resolution of the problems. The product is excellent, and I am grateful for the bonus. These problems do occur, and I appreciate that you took the effort to fix it. Continue your fantastic effort!

Very best, Mike"

Relief washed over Opsy. In a prompt response, he thanked Mike for his support and understanding.

When Opsy thought back on the incident, she saw how crucial comprehensive testing is. The last-minute scramble had served as a stark reminder that making assumptions could result in expensive errors. He might prevent future mishaps and guarantee a more seamless launch procedure by taking the time to test everything completely.

Opsy realized that the voyage was far from over even as he celebrated with Jay and Maria. The product launch saga continued, and each chapter brought new lessons and challenges. Armed with the knowledge and experience gained from his latest launch, Opsy was ready to tackle whatever came next.

Chapter 8: The Unforeseen Troubles

Opsy Bee felt more prepared than ever, having learned from the last-minute panic of his previous launch. He had taken great care to plan every detail of the introduction of his new product. He'd tested his sales funnel extensively, broadened his platform, and had solid relationships with affiliates. But as prepared as he was, Opsy eventually came to the conclusion that no amount of planning could cover every eventuality. This time, his determination would be put to the test by the absence of a backup plan.

Opsy was very thrilled about a new product launch he had planned. He was sure that everything was set up for a great debut. However, as the launch date drew nearer, he discovered an unforeseen obstacle: a significant rival declared a product launch for the same day, aimed at the same demographic. Opsy's efforts were overshadowed by the excitement around the competitor's launch, and he soon realized he needed to change course.

Sensing the heat, Opsy made the decision to give Jay a call. "Jay, I'm stuck." My debut coincides with that of a significant rival, and it's hogging all the attention. How should I proceed?

Jay gave a practical response. This is when having a backup plan comes in handy, Oppa. It is important to have a backup plan for such circumstances. Is it possible to reschedule your launch or include a unique value proposition that makes you stand out?

Opsy let out a sigh. "I didn't anticipate this. I could attempt a new time, but my viewers might become confused. It might work to add value, but I have to think fast."

Jay's tone was comforting. "Opsy, you can do this. Consider what distinct value you can provide that your rival cannot. Perhaps an exclusive webinar, a special bonus, or a temporary deal. And never forget to discuss the changes in an honest manner with your audience.

Determined to save his launch, Opsy came up with a fast list of value additions. He made the decision to provide a special extra, a live session that would offer more details and tailored advice on how to use the device. He also promised an early adopters' limited-time discount in an effort to encourage prompt purchasing.

Opsy wrote a letter outlining the new advantages and outlining the adjustments for his subscribers. He stressed the benefits of sticking with his product and was open and honest about the circumstances.

"Hello to all of you.

From OpsyBee.com, it's Opsy Bee! I wanted to provide you with some great news regarding the launch of our next product. We're providing even more value in light of recent events to make sure you get the most out of this experience.

We are now offering a special live class in which I will offer more details and one-on-one coaching. We're also giving early adopters a temporary discount. I'm determined to give you the greatest possible launch experience. I appreciate your support and am looking forward to seeing you at the session!

Best regards, Opsy Bee "His audience's reaction was positive. Many customers expressed delight about the live workshop, and they valued his transparency and added value.

Among the emails, one from Jessica, a subscriber, jumped out. Hello Opsy

I appreciate the updates and the additional information. I am eager to attend the live class as it seems like a great opportunity. We sincerely appreciate your openness and flexibility. Continue your fantastic effort!

Best regards, Jessica"

Opsy experienced a sigh of relaxation and contentment. In a prompt response, he thanked Jessica for her help and urged her to watch for the launch.

On the day of launch, Opsy's plan worked. His distinctive value offerings drew in a sizable customer base in spite of the competition. Early sales were bolstered by the one-time discount and the success of the live workshop. A possible catastrophe had been averted by Opsy's flexibility and capacity to execute a backup plan, leading to a successful launch.

As she thought back on the incident, Opsy saw how crucial it was to have a backup plan. No matter how organized he was, unanticipated problems might still happen. His ability to adapt and change course allowed him to overcome these obstacles and emerge stronger.

Opsy realized that the voyage was far from over even as he celebrated with Jay and Maria. The tale of the product launch went on, with each new chapter presenting fresh insights and difficulties. Equipped with the acumen and know-how from his most recent endeavor, Opsy was prepared to take on whatever was ahead.

Chapter 9: The Unmotivated Partners

Now that he had a working contingency plan, Opsy Bee felt more ready than ever. He was prepared to use the invaluable lessons he had learned from his past launches to his upcoming major undertaking. This time, he was going to make sure everything about his launch was well thought out and done. But he soon faced another obstacle: sustaining his affiliates' enthusiasm and motivation during the launch phase.

Opsy was eager to introduce his revolutionary new invention to the public after spending months developing it. Having assembled a robust network of affiliates, he was optimistic that their backing would propel the launch to triumph. But as the launch date drew nearer, Opsy saw a concerning pattern: a large number of his affiliates were becoming disinterested and weren't actively pushing the product as much as he had intended.

Opsy made the decision to ask Maria for guidance since she was worried. Maria, although I have a strong network of affiliates and an excellent product, they don't seem to be as motivated as I would have liked. How do I maintain their interest and enthusiasm in marketing my product?

Maria had a wise reaction. "Opsy, affiliates require rewards to maintain their motivation. Have you given thought to holding a JV competition? Encouraging top performers with rewards and incentives might incite rivalry and encourage more aggressive marketing. To keep them interested, regular communication and updates are also essential.

Opsy gave a contemplative nod. "I've never run a JV contest, but I've heard of them. "How do I configure it?"

Maria described the procedure. Choose the gifts you want to give away to the top affiliates first. It may be beneficial to receive cash bonuses, first dibs on new merchandise, or even one-on-one coaching sessions.

PRODUCT LAUNCH CHAOS

Early contest announcement and frequent leaderboard updates are recommended. This maintains the affiliates' motivation and the competitiveness vibrant. Additionally, remember to stay in constant contact with your affiliates, offering advice, support, and resources.

In a hurry to keep his affiliates interested, Opsy organized a joint venture competition. For the top 10 affiliates, he offered enticing incentives including cash bonuses, first dibs on upcoming products, and one-on-one coaching sessions. He announced the contest and detailed the guidelines and rewards in an email to his affiliates.

"Hey Team,

With the forthcoming product launch, I'm thrilled to introduce our new joint venture contest! For your hard work and assistance, I would want to express my gratitude with great awards for the top ten affiliates. Cash prizes for first place are $1,000, second place is $700, and so on.

Keep checking back for frequent leaderboard changes, and don't be afraid to get in touch if you require any help or resources. Together, let's make this launch a big success!

Best regards, The Opsy Bee" His associates responded favorably and right away. Their excitement was rekindled by the possibility of winning rewards, and Opsy observed a notable rise in promotional activity. The excitement surrounding the launch increased as affiliates started distributing his goods within their networks.

Opsy highlighted the top achievers on the contest scoreboard and urged others to increase their efforts in order to maintain the momentum. In order to help affiliates maximize their promotions and reach more potential clients, he also provided tools and advice.

One email caught my attention; it was from Alex, a top-performing affiliate. "Hello Opsy

I appreciate the contest update and the excellent advice. I'm highly motivated by the competition and working hard to get to the top. Your resources and assistance have been very beneficial. Anticipating an efficacious launch!

Warm regards, Alex

Opsy experienced a rush of fulfillment. In a prompt response, he thanked Alex for his efforts and urged him to continue his excellent work.

The combined efforts of his driven affiliates paid off on launch day. Sales skyrocketed, and the product became popular very fast. Affiliates were motivated to sell the product with fresh vigor because of the excitement and competitiveness that the JV contest had generated.

After giving the event some thought, Opsy saw how crucial it is to maintain affiliates' motivation and engagement. He'd successfully transformed a possible difficulty into a strategy by keeping lines of communication open, delivering incentives, and providing regular updates.

Opsy realized that the voyage was far from over even as he celebrated with Jay and Maria. The tale of the product launch went on, with each new chapter presenting fresh insights and difficulties. Equipped with the acumen and know-how from his most recent endeavor, Opsy was prepared to take on whatever was ahead.

Chapter 10: Out of Sight, Out of Mind

Opsy Bee felt more assured than ever after implementing a JV contest successfully in his most recent launch. Due to his ability to maintain his affiliates' motivation and engagement, the launch was a huge success. But continuous communication was set to become another essential affiliate management lesson he would soon discover.

Toward the end of the competition, Opsy had seen a decline in the zeal of his affiliates. Strong promotional efforts were sparked by the initial excitement, but as the launch approached, interest declined. Opsy was determined not to let this happen with his upcoming launch, so he chose to concentrate on being in constant contact with his affiliates.

Opsy made the decision to give Jay some counsel one morning. Jay, I've seen that as my launches come to a conclusion, affiliate involvement tends to decline. How can I maintain their engagement and attention for the duration of the campaign?

Jay gave a wise remark. "Opsy, affiliates must have a sense of belonging and recognition for their contributions. Maintaining regular contact and updates is essential to keeping them interested. Communicate your progress, recognize your accomplishments, and give support. Ensure that they are aware of your unwavering support throughout the entire process.

Resolved to enhance his approach to communication, Opsy started organizing frequent updates for his affiliates. He made the decision to send out weekly emails that included encouragement, advice, and updates on his progress. Additionally, he created a private Facebook group where affiliates could converse, exchange stories, and offer assistance to one another.

With the launch date drawing near, Opsy sent out his initial email update.

"Hey Team,

I hope all is fine with you all! The big launch is only one week away, so I wanted to give you some exciting information.

We've come a long way thus far, and I'm very appreciative of your passion and diligence. Here are some salient points:

• There's a surge in the leaderboard! See who is in the top ranks by looking at the most recent standings.

• I have updated our materials to further assist you with your promotions. We're all in this together, so make sure to check out the newly redesigned affiliate tools part of our website. Please get in touch if you need help or if you have any questions.

Combined, let's make this launch the best one to date!

Best regards, psy Be a bee"

The reaction was favorable and prompt. Affiliates valued the information Opsy was providing and the sense of community it was creating. In little time at all, the exclusive Facebook group became a hive of activity, as affiliates exchanged advice, celebrated victories, and offered mutual support.

As the launch went on, Opsy kept up with its frequent updates. He recognized the accomplishments of top-performing affiliates and shared milestones, such as reaching important sales targets. To maintain the enthusiasm and drive, he also provided extra rewards like flash bonuses and mini-contests.

Opsy once got a message from Rachel, one of the affiliates. Hello Opsy

I appreciate the Facebook group and the frequent updates. Having the sense of belonging and witnessing everyone's growth has been immensely inspiring. The additional tools and assistance have had a significant impact on my promotions. Continue your fantastic effort!

Best regards, Rachel

Opsy felt a great feeling of fulfillment. In a prompt response, he thanked Rachel for her input and urged her to carry on with her fantastic work.

As she thought back on the incident, Opsy saw how crucial regular communication is. He had sustained his affiliates' excitement and spearheaded vigorous promotion activities during the launch by keeping them updated and involved.

The outcomes were evident on the launch's last day. Affiliates were kept engaged by the frequent updates and sense of community, which led to consistent sales and an extremely successful campaign. Opsy recognized that maintaining communication would be an essential component of his approach going forward because his dedication to it had paid dividends.

Opsy realized that the voyage was far from over even as he celebrated with Jay and Maria. The tale of the product launch went on, with each new chapter presenting fresh insights and difficulties. Equipped with the acumen and know-how from his most recent endeavor, Opsy was prepared to take on whatever was ahead.

Chapter 11: The Stingy Sponsor

Opsy Bee's tenacity in communicating with his affiliates has paid off, as evidenced by the enthusiasm and engagement they showed with the launch of his most recent product. But Opsy was going to encounter another obstacle in the field of affiliate management: realizing how crucial it was to fairly compensate his partners.

Opsy planned everything out in great detail as he got ready for his next launch. He had made the decision to have another JV game because he realized how important it was to keep his affiliates motivated. But when it came to deciding on the award amounts, he wavered this time. Due to financial constraints, Opsy chose to offer lesser rewards in the hopes that the recognition of victory would inspire his affiliates.

Opsy made the decision to call Maria one day to get her opinion. "Maria, I'm concerned about the money because I've organized another JV contest. I've reduced the value of the prizes. Are you comfortable with that?

Maria gave a considerate response. "Opsy, it's crucial to provide incentives, but they must be compelling enough to inspire your affiliates. Affiliates may decide it is not worth their time to work on if the prizes are too modest, especially if they have other profitable programs to concentrate on. Think about the advantages of investing in your affiliates in the long run.

Opsy thought about Maria's counsel. "I know, but the expenses continue to worry me. How can I compensate my affiliates without going over budget?

Maria recommended a methodical approach. Offering significant monetary awards is not necessary, but you should make sure they have significance. The secret is to make your affiliates feel valued and

PRODUCT LAUNCH CHAOS

appreciated. You can also provide non-monetary incentives like special access to upcoming items, individualized coaching sessions, or even accolades and shoutouts in your community.

Opsy changed his approach, listening to Maria's advise. He introduced more non-monetary incentives in addition to a minor increase in the monetary rewards. In addition to public acknowledgment in his community and on his website, he offered the top three affiliates exclusive access to new items and private coaching sessions.

Opsy composed an email announcing the revised JV competition.

"Hey Team,

I'm thrilled to share the news of our next JV contest, which will have even greater prizes! I'm grateful for all of your hard work and support, and we've added some amazing incentives:

- First place: a one-on-one coaching session, $1,500 in cash, and first dibs on our next product.

The top ten affiliates will be publicly recognized on our website and in our community. Second place will earn $1,000 in cash and an individual coaching session. Third place will receive $700 in cash and a personalized coaching session.

I appreciate your unwavering support. Together, let's make this launch a big success!

Best regards, The Opsy BeeHis affiliates responded with great positivity. Their excitement and devotion were rekindled by the combination of increased monetary rewards and other incentives. Motivated by the chance for individualized coaching and the alluring rewards, affiliates started actively pushing the program.

Among the emails, one from Chris, an affiliate, jumped out. Hello Opsy

I appreciate the revised contest information. I'm thrilled to take part because the rewards and incentives are amazing. The one-on-one coaching sessions are an excellent bonus. Anticipating an efficacious launch!

Best regards, Chris"

Opsy felt a great feeling of fulfillment. In a prompt response, he thanked Chris for his encouragement and excitement.

Improved incentives and regular communication kept affiliates inspired and involved throughout the launch. In instance, the one-on-one coaching sessions proved to be highly popular, as numerous affiliates expressed gratitude for the chance to receive direct instruction from Opsy.

The outcomes were evident on the launch's last day. Strong promotional efforts had been fueled by the higher awards and non-monetary incentives, which had produced ongoing sales and a very successful campaign. Opsy's readiness to put money into his affiliates had paid off, demonstrating how important it was to value and honor his relationships.

After giving the event some thought, Opsy saw how crucial it is to properly compensate affiliates. He had improved connections and produced better performance by providing genuine gratitude and significant rewards.

Opsy realized that the voyage was far from over even as he celebrated with Jay and Maria. The tale of the product launch went on, with each new chapter presenting fresh insights and difficulties. Equipped with the acumen and know-how from his most recent endeavor, Opsy was prepared to take on whatever was ahead.

Chapter 12: The Lost Traffic

During his product launch journey, Opsy Bee has overcome many obstacles, such as inspiring affiliates and keeping in constant contact. His most recent launch had been successful, in part because he was prepared to sufficiently invest in and compensate his partners. But as Opsy got ready for his second launch, he realized there was one important thing he still didn't know how to do: capture departure traffic.

Opsy found that a sizable percentage of his website visitors left without making a purchase, despite his best efforts. He was aware that if he could successfully capture and convert this outbound traffic, his sales would soar and his entire performance would be enhanced. Opsy made the decision to ask Jay for guidance since she was determined to deal with this problem.

Jay, I've observed that many people are visiting my website but not making a purchase. I think I'm missing out on possible clients. How can I turn more visitors into purchasers by capturing this outbound traffic?

Jay gave a sensible reply. "Opsy, engaging visitors prior to their departure is the key to garnering exit traffic. Using exit pop-ups to provide something of value in return for their email address is one efficient technique. In this manner, you can use email marketing to follow up with them even if they decide not to buy right away. To entice them to stay, you can also provide a free resource or a temporary discount.

Opsy gave a contemplative nod. "Exit pop-ups are something I've seen before, but I've never felt comfortable using them. I don't want to aggravate my guests.

Jay gave him comfort. It all depends on how you employ them. Make sure your exit pop-ups are useful, pertinent, and don't bother you too much. If you concentrate on providing your visitors with something that actually helps them, they are more likely to enjoy it.

With the intention of successfully executing this tactic, Opsy got to work developing an exit pop-up for his website. In exchange for the email addresses of visitors, he made the decision to give away a complimentary e-book that contained insightful and helpful recommendations about his product. In addition, he put up a time-limited coupon for anyone who weren't sure whether to buy.

Opsy made sure the pop-up message was interesting and pertinent by carefully crafting it:

"Hold on! Prior to leaving...

Get our special e-book, filled with insightful advice, for free! Just fill up the email address field below.

Take advantage of a temporary 10% discount on your purchase as well! At checkout, enter the coupon SAVE10.

Don't pass up these fantastic deals!"

He configured the pop-up to appear when users indicate that they want to exit the website, and he double-checked that everything functioned as intended.

Opsy experienced a mixture of anxious expectation and excitement as the launch date drew near. Although he was aware of the potential impact of this new approach, he was uncertain about the tourists' reaction.

Opsy kept a tight eye on the exit pop-up's performance on launch day. The outcomes were positive and evident right away. Now, a lot of people who were about to exit the website without buying anything were choosing to accept the free e-book instead, then using the coupon code to finish their transaction.

One email that stuck out was from Laura, a new subscriber. Hello Opsy

I appreciate the discount code and the complimentary e-book! I decided to buy your product because of the price and the really useful advice in the e-book. Continue your fantastic effort!

Best regards, Laura

Opsy experienced a rush of fulfillment. In a brief response, he thanked Laura for her input and said he appreciated her help.

After giving the incident some thought, Opsy saw how crucial it was to record exit traffic. He had increased the number of visitors who became customers and dramatically increased his revenues by providing worthwhile incentives and judiciously utilizing exit pop-ups.

The exit pop-up performed admirably during the launch, assisting Opsy in collecting a significant amount of email addresses and bringing in more revenue. The tactic has changed the game and demonstrated how important it is to interact with visitors before they leave the website.

The outcomes were evident on the launch's last day. In order to increase conversions and drive revenue, the exit pop-up was essential. Once again, Opsy's openness to experimenting and his emphasis on adding value had paid off.

Opsy realized that the voyage was far from over even as he celebrated with Jay and Maria. The tale of the product launch went on, with each new chapter presenting fresh insights and difficulties. Equipped with the acumen and know-how from his most recent endeavor, Opsy was prepared to take on whatever was ahead.

Chapter 13: The Deflated Dream

Opsy Bee was ecstatic about his most recent launch's success and his clever usage of exit pop-ups. His confidence was skyrocketing as he got ready to launch his next product, but he was about to get a sobering reminder that even well-laid plans may go horribly wrong. Opsy felt disheartened and doubted his skills after the launch didn't proceed as planned, despite his careful planning.

Opsy had dedicated his entire being to creating a novel product, believing it would revolutionize the field of digital marketing. He had spoken with his affiliates, rigorously tested the sales funnel, and generated a great deal of pre-launch buzz. Everything appeared to be flawless.

Opsy anxiously awaited the first sales figures on launch day. He was disappointed by the lackluster response. Sales were much short of his expectations, coming in slowly. It became evident that the launch was not the triumph he had hoped for as the hours stretched into days.

Dejected, Opsy picked up the phone to ask Maria for guidance. Maria, I'm not sure I get it. Despite my best efforts, the launch was a complete failure. I'm feeling quite upset and wondering if this is the right path for me.

Maria gave a forceful yet sympathetic reaction. "Opsy, it's normal to feel let down, but failing is a necessary part of the process. Every prosperous business owner experiences obstacles. It's critical to grow from these experiences rather than allowing them to define who you are. Step back, assess what went wrong, and seize the chance to make improvements.

Determining to take lessons from the experience, Opsy made the decision to carry out an extensive post-launch analysis. He contacted Jay to get further information.

PRODUCT LAUNCH CHAOS

The launch didn't go as expected, Jay. I'm attempting to determine what went wrong. Any suggestions on how to handle this?

Jay gave a sensible reply. "Opsy, begin by getting input from your affiliates and clients. Examine your data to determine the locations of drop-offs. Did your message make an impression? Did you overlook any technical issues? Make use of this data to pinpoint places that need work. Recall that every setback presents a chance for growth.

Opsy took Jay's advice and started getting input. He requested candid feedback on what worked and what didn't in surveys that he distributed to his affiliates and clients. In order to find any possible problems, he also dug into his website analytics and carefully examined every stage of the sales funnel.

The comments were instructive. In comparison to other similar products on the market, several customers complained that the pricing was excessive. Some noted that expectations were raised by the pre-launch material, which the finished product fell short of. Affiliates pointed out that the marketing materials should have done a better job of grabbing readers' attention and highlighting the advantages of the product.

With this important knowledge in hand, Opsy got to work improving. He changed the product's content to better meet customer expectations and changed the pricing structure to provide more value for the money. Additionally, he updated the marketing materials to emphasize the best qualities of the offering.

Opsy started to see a bright side when he put these modifications into practice. He had learned a valuable lesson from the first disaster, which he could apply to this and subsequent product launches. He came to see that failures were an unavoidable aspect of being an entrepreneur and that the secret to long-term success was perseverance and adaptation.

Opsy once got an email from a client called David. Hello Opsy

We appreciate your follow-up and your consideration of our suggestions. I value your commitment to making the product better. You made some really great modifications, and I'm delighted I gave it another go. Continue moving forward!

Best regards, David

Opsy was filled with a fresh resolve. In a prompt response, he thanked David for his advice and encouragement.

When Opsy thought back on the incident, she saw how crucial resilience is when facing setbacks. His ability to see setbacks as chances for improvement and education had allowed him to turn a bad start into a worthwhile one.

Opsy realized that the voyage was far from over even as he celebrated with Jay and Maria. The tale of the product launch went on, with each new chapter presenting fresh insights and difficulties. Equipped with the acumen and know-how from his most recent endeavor, Opsy was prepared to take on whatever was ahead.

PRODUCT LAUNCH CHAOS

Chapter 14: Ignoring the Lessons

Opsy Bee's path in the realm of product introductions had been an emotional rollercoaster. Every launch taught fresh lessons, and he had developed from his past to become adaptive. But Opsy made a crucial error as he got ready for yet another product release: he neglected the knowledge he had diligently acquired.

Fresh off the heels of his last release, Opsy was sure. Having perfected the craft of product introduction, he chose to speed the introduction of his next product. Thinking he could simplify the process and yet produce outstanding results, he avoided numerous phases that had earlier been very vital.

Opsy relied more on his instincts about what his audience desired than on careful market research. He also hurried through the pre-launch stage, thinking the product would be carried by his established name. Moreover, he disregarded the requirement of thorough testing since he thought his experience would solve any possible problems.

Opsy decided one evening as the launch day drew near to call Maria to let her know he was excited. Maria, I have simplified the launch process for this. I have great hope it will be popular. To save time, I have cut back on a lot of the getting ready.

Maria responded carefully. "Opsy, while your confidence is admirable, don't overlook the need of preparation." Every stage of the procedure serves a purpose. Igniting them could cause unanticipated issues. Are you absolutely not missing anything?

Opsy ignored her worries. Maria: "I have this. I know what I am doing; I have done this before. I simply need this product on the market.

PRODUCT LAUNCH CHAOS

Opsy was both excited and terrified as the launch day dawned. The first answer was indifferent, and it was evident as the day went on that something was off. Customer comments revealed various problems with the product and the launch technique; sales were much below projected.

Experiencing a déjà vu, Opsy chose to consult Jay for guidance. "Jay, the launch is not proceeding according. Though it seems like I made some blunders, I believed I had everything worked out. What then ought I to do?

Jay answered squarely. "Opsy, it sounds like you could have missed some important phases. Have you looked extensively at the market? Did your audience participate during the pre-launch period? Have you appropriately tested everything?

Opsy sighed, seeing he missed something. "No, I cut those steps to save time. I assumed I could depend on experience.

Jay spoke with strength yet encouragement. "Although experience is great, it cannot substitute careful planning. Every launch is different; skipping steps can cause problems. Every experience should teach us something, hence we should always utilize those knowledge. Consider this as a teaching moment and ensure to use the procedure the next time.

Driven to correct his errors, Opsy chose to grab anything he could from the launch. He answered questions from his clients and provided more tools and help. Additionally he spent time compiling thorough comments, which he applied right away to improve the product.

Opsy emailed his clients noting the problems and providing fixes.

"Hi everyone,

I am appreciative of your patience and support. After reading your comments, I am carefully working to solve the problems. I'm providing extra tools and help to demonstrate my gratitude and guarantee you maximize this product. I appreciate your understanding; I am determined to right this.

Excellent, Oesy Bee" His clients responded politely, and many valued his candor and readiness for change.

One email especially noteworthy came from a client called Sarah. " Hi Opsy,

I appreciate you handling the problems and providing further help. I value your will to enhance the offering. I'm sure it would be even better right now. Maintaining your excellent effort is great!

Ideal, Sarah'

Opsy came out determined once more. Quickly responding, he thanked Sarah for her comments and encouragement.

When he thought back on the encounter, Opsy understood how crucial it was to regularly implement the knowledge he had gained. He had risked his launch and his reputation by omitting vital stages. He promised himself going ahead to strictly follow the procedure so that every launch was carefully scheduled and carried out.

Opsy understood the trip was far from finished as he celebrated with Maria and Jay. The story of the product introduction carried fresh difficulties and insights in every chapter. Equipped with the wisdom from his most recent launch, Opsy was prepared to face whatever was ahead.

Chapter 15: The Halfway Halt

Recent events for Opsy Bee have shown him realize the value of constancy and readiness. He was resolved to implement all he had learnt as he got ready for his next product release. From market research to pre-launch involvement, he painstakingly scheduled every element and felt sure this launch would be his finest yet. But Opsy was about to face a fresh obstacle that would try his fortitude—the will to keep going midway through the process.

Designed to assist digital marketers to simplify their campaigns and obtain better results, the new offering was an advanced marketing toolbox. Opsy had poured his heart and soul into every element as he worked months creating the toolset. Sharing it with the public thrilled him, and he felt sure it would revolutionize his clients.

Opsy had a run of unanticipated difficulties as the launch date drew near. Technical problems dogged the sales funnel, and even with his best efforts, they persisted. Those who had first shown great excitement about the project started to drop out, pointing other obligations. The pre-launch participation was meager, and Opsy started to feel frustrated and doubtful.

Overwhelmed one evening, Opsy chose to call Maria for guidance. Maria, this launch is causing me so many problems. Technical issues won't go away; associates are leaving; pre-launch activity is not as robust as I had planned. I'm beginning to feel as though I ought just give up.

Maria answered with tenacity and encouragement. "Opsy, every launch comes with difficulties." The vital thing is not to give up. Recall that those who tenaciously pursue even if it seems unattainable usually find success. Back off, evaluate the circumstances, and then work out answers. Yougone too far to give up right now.

Resolved to keep on, Opsy chose to ask Jay for extra help. Jay, I am somewhat demoralized right now. There are so many challenges ahead of the launch that I could find myself tempted to give up. What then ought I to do?

Jay spoke gently and with encouragement. "Opsy, the road calls for both setbacks. Your reaction to them counts most. If you must take breaks, do so; however, never give up. One issue at a time, concentrate on it steadily. You can do it; you have already conquered a great deal.

Inspired by their counsel, Opsy resolved to take on the problems squarely. He began by addressing the technical issues and working with a reputable developer to troubleshoot and mend the sales funnel. He then contacted his surviving associates, providing further incentives and support to keep them involved.

Opsy also changed his pre-launch plan and produced fresh, interesting material to spark enthusiasm and interest once more Offering insightful analysis and first looks at the toolset, he organized a number of live webinars The answer was good, and involvement started to pick up.

One day Opsy got an email from Mark, an affiliate. "Hi Opsy,"

I value your extra help and the interesting webinars. Though the technological problems were aggravating, I value your commitment to fixing them. I am back on board eager to advertise the toolbox. Let's make this launch successful.

Best, Mark Mark"

Opsy had a fresh will. He answered fast, thanks Mark for his support and expressing appreciation for his dedication.

Opsy had both anxiety and exhilaration as the launch day drew near. Notwithstanding the challenges, he had persisted and his efforts were going to pay off. The first sales were robust, and consumer comments were overwhelmingly favorable. The sophisticated marketing toolset was a hit, and Opsy's fortitude had turned possible failure into a loud success.

When she thought back on the encounter, Opsy understood the need of tenacity. He had reached his objectives by not giving up and systematically tackling every obstacle. Though the road had been challenging, the lessons gained were priceless.

Opsy understood the trip was far from finished as he celebrated with Maria and Jay. The story of the product introduction carried fresh difficulties and insights in every chapter. Equipped with the wisdom from his most recent launch, Opsy was prepared to face whatever happened next.

Chapter 16: Quality Over Quantity

Opsy Bee's recent success gave him fresh hope for his capacity to manage the many obstacles of product introductions. Riding high on the success of his sophisticated marketing toolbox, he felt prepared for on next major assignment. Opsy was about to discover, nevertheless, a vital lesson about the value of product quality above mere volume.

Opsy chose to intensify his efforts on product creation in line with his increased success. He imagined a range of smaller, specialized goods targeted at several digital marketing niches. With an eye toward a large audience, the concept was to inundate the market with several offerings. Opsy started working on numerous items concurrently in his haste to grab on to his momentum.

One evening Opsy decided to call Maria for guidance while juggling several projects. "Maria, I'm working on numerous concurrently new projects. This is a fantastic approach, in my opinion, to increase my reach and depict several business sectors. What do you suppose?

Maria's reply was measured. "Opsy, your ambition is fantastic, but be careful not to compromise quality for volume." Rushing through several projects can produce unsatisfactory goods and unhappy consumers. Emphasize providing excellent items even if it means introducing fewer products.

Opsy nodded, but he was resolved to move ahead with his scheme. His experience and recent accomplishment, he thought, would help him going forward. But he started to produce less as he kept juggling several tasks. He discovered he was sacrificing quality in order to reach deadlines, and the final items fell short of his expectations.

One afternoon Opsy got an email from Lisa, an early customer. " Hello Opsy,

PRODUCT LAUNCH CHAOS

I have to admit, I'm dissatisfied after lately buying one of your new goods. The material seems hurried, and a number of mistakes make it challenging. Although your work is generally of quality, this one falls short of my expectations.

Best, Lisa:

Opsy started to feel guilty. He came to see he had overlooked the quality that had won him a devoted following in his haste to create several things. Driven to right things, Opsy chose to ask Jay for guidance.

"Jay, I made a mistake. I sacrificed quality in order to concentrate too much on quantity. Negative comments I get are compromising my reputation. What then ought I to do?

Jay answered with a direct approach. "Opsy, you're lucky to identify the problem. First, contact your clients and provide replacements or refunds to attend to the current issues. Step back then and give quality top priority above quantity. Emphasize on producing less but better products. Your reputation relies on it.

Determined to right things, Opsy moved right away. Apologizing emails to his consumers, he offered replacements or refunds and admitted the problems with the most recent products.

"hi everyone,

I would want to apologies for the lately unsatisfactory products. Thank you for your comments; I am acting right away to solve the problems. Tell me if you're unhappy; I will provide a replacement or a complete return. First concern is your satisfaction.

I appreciate your perspective.

Good, Opsy Bee." much

His clients responded with understanding; many valued his candor and readiness to put things right. One email especially noteworthy came from a client called Karen. "Hello Opsy,

I appreciate your fast reply and resolution of the problems. I value your commitment to excellence and consumer happiness. Your next products will much be awaited.

Perfect, Karen

Opsy redoubled her efforts toward direction. He answered fast, appreciating Karen's help and pledging going forward to provide better products.

When Opsy thought back on the encounter, she understood how crucial it was to keep great standards. Emphasizing quality above quantity will help him to make sure every item satisfied his consumers and maintained his brand.

Opsy understood the road was far from finished as he celebrated with Maria and Jay. The story of the product introduction carried fresh difficulties and insights in every chapter. Equipped with the wisdom from his most recent launch, Opsy was prepared to face whatever happened next.

Chapter 17: The Silent Channel

Over his path of product introductions, Opsy Bee had acquired numerous insightful knowledge; the most recent one was the need of quality above quantity. Opsy felt ready for his next assignment, focused once more and committed to upholding high standards. Still, one crucial component of contemporary marketing he had not really embraced—social media. His resistance to use social media strategically was about to be tested.

Opsy had always been wary to enter social media, even with his achievements. He thought traditional email marketing and affiliate promotions were enough to generate sales, hence he favored them. But it became evident as the digital terrain changed that social media was a potent instrument with which one could not overlook.

Opsy resolved one afternoon to phone Maria to go over his forthcoming launch. "Maria, I have been avoiding social media even though my next product excites me. Do you suppose I really should commit time and money to it?

Maria answered with great vigor. "Opsy, engaging your audience and generating excitement around your items depend on social media. It's a means of attracting fresh clients, fostering relationships, and maintaining brand top-of-mind integrity. Though you are not on every platform, having a strong presence on one or two will make a significant difference.

Opsy nodded slowly. Social networking has always made me feel overburdles. Where will I begin?

Maria's counsel made sense. "Start with the venues your audience most visits. Emphasize producing interesting material with value, highlights your knowledge, and strengthens your relationship with your readers.

One must be consistent. Social media ads can also be used to target particular groups and increase website visitors for your sales pages.

Driven to venture outside his comfort zone, Opsy chose to concentrate on Facebook and Instagram, sites where his target market was likely to be found. He started by developing a content calendar, organizing pieces ranging from advertising teasers and customer quotes to instructional materials and behind-the-scenes peeks.

Opsy has opted to communicate personally with his audience by doing a series of live Q&A sessions on Facebook, therefore providing insightful analysis. By email and on social media, he encouraged his fans to attend and take part in these sessions.

One evening Opsy got a note from Emma, a follower. "Hello Opsy,

I joined the last live Q&A session after following your Facebook postings. I wanted to thank you for the interactive seminars and the worthwhile material. Your social media interaction with your audience is fantastic. Looking forward your future product introduction!

Excellent, Emma is"

Opsy came away feeling successful. Reacting fast, he expressed his enthusiasm about the forthcoming release and thanked Emma for her support.

Opsy saw a notable rise in excitement and involvement around his invention as the launch date drew near. Consistent social media posts, live sessions, and targeted ads taken together generated excitement and expectation for his following.

On launch day, Opsy's social media plan worked. Strong sales accompanied by overwhelming good consumer reaction. Many said they

PRODUCT LAUNCH CHAOS

found the product via his social media activity and valued the interesting connections and material.

When she thought back on the event, Opsy saw how important social media is to contemporary marketing. Through efficient use of various channels, he had expanded his audience, developed close relationships, and raised his sales.

One email especially noteworthy came from a client called Tom. After seeing your Instagram posts, Hi Opsy decided to attend your live Q&A events. I'm happy with my purchase and found great use for your insights. I appreciate your being so approachable and interesting on social media.

Perfect, Tom"

Opsy experienced a great degree of gratification. Responding fast, he thanked Tom for his comments and expressed thanks for the help.

Opsy understood the road was far from finished as he celebrated with Maria and Jay. The story of the product introduction carried fresh difficulties and insights in every chapter. Equipped with the wisdom from his most recent launch, Opsy was prepared to face whatever happened next.

Chapter 18: The Unforeseen Troubles

Opsy Bee's success including social media into his marketing plan has given him a different viewpoint on contemporary digital marketing. With every new product release, he was anxious to keep developing his method and inventing. Opsy was about to encounter a set of unanticipated problems, though, that would try his tenacity and flexibility even with his exacting preparation.

Opsy's next offering was a thorough video course covering advanced email marketing techniques. Having spent many hours creating excellent material, he felt sure the course would be popular. Drawing on past launches, he had also applied lessons to guarantee that everything from the pre-launch buzz to the affiliate involvement was carefully scheduled.

Opsy started to run over unanticipated difficulties nevertheless, as the launch date drew near. First, a major affiliate who had pledged notable advertising support withdrew at last minute owing to a personal crisis. Opsy had relied on the reach of this affiliate to produce most of his sales, hence this was a major loss.

Under duress, Opsy chose to call Jay for guidance. "Jay, one of my best friends just withdrew, and I'm concerned about how the launch may be impacted. What am I supposed to do?

Jay answered with a cool head and assurance. "Opsy, the game consists in unexpected challenges. Pay attention to your controllable factors. Ask other associates, even ones you would not have first thought of. Give them extra benefits to board. Additionally consider stepping up your social media campaigns to offset the decreased reach.

Determined to change, Opsy promptly got in touch with associates, giving them extra bonuses and more commissions for advertising his

PRODUCT LAUNCH CHAOS

goods. To create more buzz, he also stepped up his social media activities, running focused advertising and interacting more directly with his fans.

Another problem developed just as Opsy began to feel more in control. A technical flaw in his sales funnel let some clients run across issues throughout the checkout process. Emails and panicked texts began pouring in, and Opsy knew he had to respond quickly.

Overwhelmed, Opsy chose to call Maria for direction. "Maria, consumers are having problems checking out and I have a technical sales funnel issue. How fast enough I should fix it is unknown."

Maria answered with a sensible approach. First, Opsy, interact with your clients. Tell them you know of the problem and are working on it. To further troubleshoot and fix the issue, then contact a reliable developer or your technical support crew. As a means of apologies and keeping their goodwill, provide impacted consumers a unique discount or bonus.

Following Maria's counsel, Opsy sent an email to his clients right away noting the problem and extending a courtesy temporary discount.

" hello everyone,

I wish to apologies for the technical problems the checkout process brought about. We are actively trying to find a solution as fast as feasible. Thank you for your patience; kindly apply a 10% discount on your order using the SORRY10 code. We value your understanding and backing.

Excellent, Ozzy Bee""

He subsequently got in touch with his technical support staff, who toiled nonstop to find and remedy the flaw. The problem was fixed a few hours later, and the sales funnel was once more working without problems.

One email especially noteworthy came from a client called Mike. "Hi Opsy,"

I appreciate the discount and for you immediately fixing the technical problem. I value your candor and fast response. Getting into the course excites me!

Best, Mike:"

Opsy was in relief and thanks. Responding fast, he thanked Mike for his understanding and encouragement.

When she thought back on the event, Opsy saw how crucial it is to be ready for unanticipated problems. He had negotiated the difficulties and maintained his launch on schedule by remaining cool, honest, and fast in adaptation.

Sales picked significantly as the launch went on, and client comments were generally favorable. Opsy's tenacity and fast thinking had turned possible tragedies into chances for development and education in spite of the losses.

Ozzy knew the road was far from finished as he rejoiced with Maria and Jay. The story of the product introduction carried fresh difficulties and insights in every chapter. Equipped with the wisdom from his most recent launch, Opsy was prepared to face whatever happened next.

Chapter 19: Unwillingness to Reward Partners

Opsy Bee had seen many storms on his path across the realm of product introductions. Technical problems, unexpected difficulties, and the need of upholding high standards had all come under his purview. But one lesson he was about to learn—the need of kindly praising his associates and partners—would prove vital for his long-term success.

Opsy felt sure in his approach as he got ready for his next product introduction. From the marketing campaign to the product development, he had painstakingly coordinated every element. Opsy hesitated, though, about determining commission rates and incentives for his associates. Concerned about cutting into his earnings, he chose to provide below-average commissions.

Feeling doubtful one evening, Opsy decided to phone Maria for guidance. "Maria, although I'm getting ready for the upcoming launch, the large commission fees worry me. To preserve my margins, I have set the rates smaller. Do you find that to be a wise concept?

Maria answered, and her response was assessed. "Opsy, while controlling your expenses is vital, encouraging your associates depends on providing competitive commissions. Should they feel underappreciated, they might not commit the necessary energy to properly advertise your goods. Think about the long-term advantages of large commissions—stronger ties with associates and maybe more sales volume.

Opsy nodded quietly. "I know, but finding the right balance is difficult. What ought I to do?

Maria advised a methodical approach with balances. "Think about providing a tiered commission plan. Offer top performers increased rates starting with a competitive base rate. In this sense, you still control your total expenses while rewarding the top sales drivers. Consider non-financial incentives as well, such as special recognition or first access to upcoming goods.

Opsy changed his commission plan, resolved to strike the proper mix. He decided to provide top-performing associates higher pay and a base rate competitive with industry standards. He also included non-financial incentives, early access to new goods and unique website and social media acknowledgment.

Opsy sent an email announcing the revised commission schedule and incentives.

hello Team,

Announcing our forthcoming product release and the new commission plan meant to honor your effort and support excites me. You should anticipate:

- Base commission: thirty percent.

- Tiered bonuses for top performers: up to 50% for those with maximum sales

Exclusive access to upcoming items; special acknowledgment on our website and social media

I appreciate your ongoing patronage. Let's make this launch a great success team effort!

Better still, Oggy Bee"

His associates responded right away and positively. The competitive commissions and extra incentives sparked once more their zeal and

PRODUCT LAUNCH CHAOS

dedication. Driven by the appealing benefits and chance for recognition, affiliates started vigorously advertising the product.

One email particularly noteworthy came from Rachel, a top-performing affiliate. "Hi Opsy,

I appreciate the changed commission structure and the extra incentives. Excellent are the tiered benefits and early access to upcoming goods. Promoting this launch and aiming for the highest tier excites me. Let's go at this!

ideal, Rachel

Opsy experienced great gratification. He answered fast, appreciating Rachel's support and thanks for her commitment.

The help of his associates was overwhelming as the launch day approached. Strong advertising campaigns powered by the kind commission system and other incentives have resulted in a sales explosion. The good comments from clients and the active participation of associates 4o ChatGPT justified Opsy's choice to make investments in his partners.

When she thought back on the encounter, Opsy understood how much he should value and reward his associates. Offering competitive commissions and other incentives, he had developed closer ties and produced greater results. Investing in his associates paid off long-term significantly more than the initial expenses.

Opsy once got an email from an affiliate called Tom. " Hello Opsy,

I wanted to thank you for the honor and the kind commissions. Knowing that our efforts are valued and rewarded motivates us. Working with you on next releases excites me. Maintain the fantastic work.

optimal, Tom,"

Opsy was once more fulfilled. Responding fast, he thanked Tom for his comments and expressed thanks for his support.

The sales kept rising as the launch went on, and consumer comments were overwhelmingly good. The product was a hit, and Opsy's readiness to treat his colleagues had been very important in its popularity.

Opsy understood the trip was far from finished as he celebrated with Maria and Jay. The story of the product launch carried fresh difficulties and insights in every chapter. Equipped with the wisdom and experience from his most recent launch, Opsy was prepared to face whatever was ahead.

Chapter 20: The Blind Eye to Competition

On his path of product introductions, Opsy Bee had gained a great deal of knowledge about Though he was more ready than ever for his next trip, he still lacked one vital knowledge—the need of knowing and reacting to competition. Opsy neglected the competitive environment as he concentrated on creating his newest product, a mistake he would soon find haunting him.

Opsy's latest offering was a thorough manual on cutting-edge advanced content marketing techniques. He thought it would close a market gap and was sure of its worth. He gave his all to improve the material, interact with associates, and create buzz before launch. He did not, however, thoroughly investigate his rivals and missed a similar product set for launch at the same time.

Ozzy got a call from Jay one evening. "Opsy, have you lately looked at the competitiveness? I had heard of a brand-new product arriving that fairly closely resembles yours. You might like to look at it.

Opsy pouted. "I have not had time since I have been so preoccupied with my own endeavor. What size of a problem do you believe this to be?

Jay answered softly, wary. "It might be important. Understanding what your rivals have to offer will enable you to showcase the special value of your product and set it apart. Though you must move fast, it is not too late to make corrections.

Driven to grasp the competitive scene, Opsy investigated his rivals over the next few hours. He found that a well-known marketer with a sizable following and notable pre-launch hype was introducing a related product. Though it contained some distinct bonuses that enhanced its appeal, the competitor's product had many of the same features and advantages as Opsy's.

Under pressed, Opsy chose to ask Maria for guidance. "Maria, I recently found out that a big rival is introducing a related product. They have some unusual bonuses and great buzz. What action ought I to do?

Maria responded pragmatically. "Opsy, you really must set your product apart. Emphasize the specialness and value of your guide. Could you add any special benefits or features not offered by your rival company? Furthermore take into account immediately addressing the competition in your marketing to demonstrate why your product is the better option.

Determined to act, Opsy nodded. He considered methods to improve his offering and chose to include a set of special webinars including guest content marketing specialists. He also supplied a unique supplemental e-book with more ideas and techniques not included in the primary guide.

Opsy changed his marketing materials fast to highlight these special qualities and the extra value his product offers. He sent an email to his customers stressing the improvements and the reasons his product set out from the others.

"Hello, everyone.

It gives me great pleasure to present some amazing updates on our forthcoming product release! We have included special bonus e-books loaded with more ideas and techniques and exclusive webinars featuring renowned content marketing professionals. This is why our guide is the greatest one available to you:

• Special insights from business leaders; • Exclusive extra material not found anywhere else.

PRODUCT LAUNCH CHAOS

- Complete plans catered to your circumstances

Don't overlook these incredible characteristics! I appreciate your ongoing support.

Ideally, Ozzy Bee"His audience answered right away and favorably. The extra value and special qualities sparked their enthusiasm and curiosity once more. Opsy also executed a focused advertising campaign stressing the improvements, therefore reaching a larger audience and creating more buzz.

One particularly noteworthy email came from Laura, a subscriber. " Hi Opsy,

I like the bonus additions and updates. Excellent additions include the webinars including guest speakers and the complimentary e-book. Having your guide in hand now makes me even more eager. Maintain the excellent effort.

Optimal, Laura.

Opsy became even more determined. Responding fast, he said he appreciated Laura's passion and thanked her for her support.

Oggy's approach paid off on launch day. Notwithstanding the rivalry, his product attracted good reviews and significant sales. The special qualities and additional value had distinguished his guide and demonstrated how important it is to grasp and react to the competitive environment.

When she thought back on the event, Opsy understood how crucial competitor analysis was. Staying current with the market and differentiating his product had helped him to turn a possible setback into a successful launch.

Opsy knew the trip was far from done as he rejoiced with Maria and Jay. The story of the product release went on, and every chapter presented fresh obstacles and lessons. Equipped with the information and expertise acquired from his most recent launch, Opsy was prepared to face whatever was ahead.

Chapter 21: Ignoring Client Comment

Opsy Bee's confidence had been raised by his recent accomplishment differentiating his products in a cutthroat industry. He had discovered the need of keeping current with the competition and of providing special value to his products. But Opsy was about to pick still another vital lesson: the need of paying close attention to and using client comments.

Opsy has always taken great satisfaction in producing excellent goods fit for his market. But in his pursuit of excellence, he sometimes ignored direct client comments as he thought he knew best. He stayed true to his own instincts without consulting his consumers as he got ready for his next product release, a complete social media marketing toolset.

One evening Opsy was finishing the product details when he got a note from a devoted customer called Karen. Hi Opsy,

Having used your products for some time now, I have always valued your effort. But I thought your current social media marketing material may use additional case studies and real-world examples. Simply said: keep up the excellent effort!

Best, Karen"

Opsy skimmed the message, but he was too preoccupied with his upcoming launch to pay close attention. He thought his method was strong and saw no need for including Karen's recommendation. He proceeded with his plans, sure his experience would show.

Opsy saw that pre-launch involvement was below average as the launch date drew near. Though he made a lot of marketing, the buzz and excitement around the product lacked the force he had anticipated. Slightly worried, he chose to give Jay some guidance over the phone.

" Jay, for this launch I am seeing less participation than usual. Though I have worked as hard, something seems off. What do you think?

Jay responded deliberately. "Opsy, have you thought of getting more direct comments from your readers? Sometimes we become so engross in our own ideas that we overlook the genuine needs of our clients. Have you included comments into this product?

Ozzy stopped. "I got some comments, but I didn't feel it necessary to modify my strategy. You believe that to be the problem?

Jay spoke in a forceful voice. "Opsy, you really must listen to your clients. Their comments can offer insightful analysis not something you would have thought about. You have time to change. Ask your audience for comments, then demonstrate to them your appreciation of their points of view.

Driven to turn things around, Opsy chose to follow Jay's counsel. Seeking comments and ideas on what they wanted in the new toolbox, he contacted his email list and social media following. He also went back over Karen's advice and chose to include more case studies and real-world examples into the offering.

Opsy sent an email to his members encouraging them to offer comments.

" Hi everyone,

I would value your comments as I am developing an interesting new toolkit for social media marketing. I really appreciate your help; therefore, I want to make sure this product satisfies your requirements. With social media marketing, what toughest obstacles must you overcome? Of what qualities would you most benefit?

I value your opinions and support. We can produce something quite remarkable together!

Excellent, Ozzy Bee"

The answer came right away and was astounding. Consumers were happy to have their opinions sought for and ready to offer them. Opsy got a lot of comments pointing up typical difficulties and suggesting elements that would make the toolbox more valuable.

One email especially noteworthy came from a client called Jake. "Hello Opsy,

We appreciate your seeking of our opinions. Locating actual case studies of effective social media advertising is one of the toughest tasks I have. Your toolkit would be much benefited by include case studies and useful examples. Anticipating the last work result!

Superior, Javier"

Opsy redoubled her search for meaning. He answered fast, thanks Jake for his comments and reassured him the toolkit would feature more useful case studies and examples.

Opsy found the material much improved as he included the comments into his creation. The case studies and practical examples gave the toolkit additional value and depth, therefore increasing its relevance to his readers.

The launch day results spoke for themselves. Sales and participation were far higher than expected, and client comments were unanimously good. Opsy had produced a product that really fit his consumers by paying attention to their comments.

When she thought back on the encounter, Opsy came to see how important client comments were. He had improved his product and enhanced his relationship with his audience by aggressively searching for and including their ideas.

Opsy understood the trip was far from finished as he celebrated with Maria and Jay. The story of the product introduction carried fresh difficulties and insights in every chapter. Equipped with the wisdom from his most recent launch, Opsy was prepared to face whatever happened next.

Chapter 22: Overestimating the Market

By learning to listen to consumer comments and adjust, Opsy Bee has effectively negotiated the complexity of product launches. He felt more capable and confident with every release. His next difficulty, though, would come from another direction—misjudging the scale and preparedness of his target market.

Opsy chose to build a premium membership site with unique tools, resources, and content for skilled digital marketers for his next endeavor. He made large investments in site development, content creation, and marketing materials since he felt there was a great market for such a thorough, high-value product. He expected many sign-ups since he was certain the high price point would be justified by the value given.

Opsy phoned Maria to let her know he was becoming excited about the launch day. Maria, this new membership website excites me greatly. I have put a lot of money into it and am sure it will be quite successful. I think this kind of luxury product has a strong market.

Maria answered with encouragement but also caution. "Opsy, although it sounds like a great initiative, have you checked the market demand for a membership this expensive? Sometimes our passion could skew our judgment. It is imperative to make sure a sizable market ready to pay for this product exists.

Opsy nodded, but he was sure of his opinion. "Based on some study, I believe the market is large enough. It will definitely be a success.

On the debut day, Opsy excitedly awaited the sign-ups. But it became abundantly evident as the hours went by that the answer fell far short of his expectations. Very few customers were ready to pay the extra price despite the excellent material and extensive tools. Opsy came to see he had overstated the market's capacity for such a high-priced product's demand and willingness to make such investments.

Disappointed, Opsy decided to give Jay guidance on calls. "Jay, the launch is not going smoothly. Although I believed this membership site had a strong market, the sign-ups are far lower than I anticipated. Which mistake did I make?

Jay gave a simple answer. "Opsy, you might have overstated the demand for the market." Before extensively funding a project, you should confirm your presumptions with extensive market research and testing. Pivoting still has time. To draw more consumers, think about providing a less expensive range or extra value.

Resolved to turn things around, Opsy chose to follow Jay's counsel. In order to provide access to a range of the premium content and features, he swiftly unveiled a less expensive tier for the membership site In an effort to encourage sign-up, he also included a limited-time discount for new members.

Opsy sent his members an email introducing the new tier and discount.

"Hi everybody,

We appreciate your showing of interest in our new membership website. To make our unique materials more easily available, we have added a new, less expensive level. You may also benefit from a limited-time exclusive membership discount. Come now and grab these amazing deals!

Best, Opsy Bee"

The answer came right away and was favorable. Many members who had put off joining at the premium pricing point were now keen to register for the more reasonably priced solution. Discount and lower-priced tiers helped to boost site interaction and sign-up numbers.

PRODUCT LAUNCH CHAOS

One email particularly noteworthy came from a new member called Alex. "Hi Ozzy,

I appreciate you proposing the discount and the additional tier. Though I couldn't justify the premium payment, I wanted to join your membership website. I could join with the new choices, and the material is incredibly appealing. Continue the outstanding work.

Greatest, Alex

Opsy was relieved and thanksgiving. He answered fast, thanks Alex for his comments and expressing gratitude for the support.

When she thought back on the experience, Opsy understood how crucial it was to fairly evaluate market demand. He had rescued his launch by verifying his presumptions and being ready to change, therefore transforming a possible disaster into a teaching tool.

Opsy knew the road was far from finished as he celebrated with Maria and Jay. The story of the product release went on, and every chapter presented fresh obstacles and lessons. Equipped with the information and expertise acquired from his most recent launch, Opsy was prepared to face whatever was ahead.

Chapter 23: Inadequate Support System

Opsy Bee's agility and adaptability had helped many of his launches escape possible catastrophe. Every each obstacle imparted priceless lessons, and he felt more ready than ever to meet whatever came his way. But his next endeavour would draw attention to a crucial point he had sometimes missed: a strong customer care system is vital.

Opsy chose to develop a suite of cutting-edge digital marketing tools for his most recent offering, combined in a complete toolbox. He spent a lot of time and money creating these instruments, sure they would be quite valuable for his clients. But he undervalued the need of giving his new and maybe complicated product enough support.

Opsy concentrated on honing the instruments and producing interesting marketing collateral as the launch date drew near. He didn't give much effort to building up a thorough support structure since he expected the caliber of the goods would be evident. Assuming that would be plenty, he established a rudimentary FAQ page and an email address for support questions.

Opsy decided one evening to phone Maria to let her know how he was doing. "Maria, the fresh digital marketing toolkit excites me. I have worked rather hard to ensure the tools are first-rate. Consumers will love it, I believe.

Maria answered with a curious yet positive attitude. "Opsy, it sounds amazing. Have you built up a thorough client assistance system? Sometimes advanced tools can be difficult to operate, hence clients could need assistance.

Opsy stopped. "I email for support and have a FAQ page. Do you believe that to be sufficient?

PRODUCT LAUNCH CHAOS 81

Maria spoke softly yet firmly. "Opsy, especially with complicated products, consumers will probably have queries and run into problems. Therefore, great support is absolutely essential to guarantee their happiness and success. Think of building a more strong support network with live chat, thorough knowledge base, maybe even video training."

Driven to make sure his clients had a great experience, Opsy chose to follow Maria's counsel. He rapidly added a live chat option to his website, developed thorough video training for every tool, and extended the FAQ area into a complete knowledge library. To answer questions and offer quick help, he also assembled a modest support staff.

Opsy sent his customers an email introducing the fresh assistance tools.

Hi everybody,

It gives me great pleasure to declare the release of our fresh toolbox for digital marketing! We have built up a thorough support system including live chat support for real-time help to guarantee you have the greatest experience.

- Comprehensive knowledge base including exacting step-by-step instructions; • Comprehensive video tutorials for every tool

Our first concern is your success; we are here to support you all through.

Good, Ozzy BeeThe "

His audience responded right away and favorably. Knowing that aid was just waiting for them if they needed it, consumers valued the extra support and felt more confidence in using the toolkit.

One email particularly noteworthy came from a new client called Julia. Hi Opsy,

I appreciate the superb support system and toolbox. Live chat and video tutorials have been really beneficial. One of the tools piqued my curiosity, thus the support staff was fast to help. Fantastic work ensuring we have the tools required!

Optimal, Julia

Opsy felt a great sense of gratification. He answered fast, thanks Julia for her comments and expressing thanks for her support.

The thorough support system proved quite helpful as the launch went forward. Those who ran across problems could get assistance right away, and the thorough training and knowledge base enabled consumers to maximize the toolbox. The good comments and high customer satisfaction confirmed the need of giving strong support.

When she thought back on the event, Opsy came to see how important customer service was to the success of a product introduction. Making sure his clients could get the assistance they required would have improved their experience and strengthened his bonds with them.

Opsy understood the road was far from finished as he celebrated with Maria and Jay. The story of the product introduction carried fresh difficulties and insights in every chapter. Equipped with the wisdom from his most recent launch, Opsy was prepared to face whatever happened next.

Chapter 24: The Overlooked Analytics

The popularity of Opsy Bee's most recent product release highlighted the need of a strong customer care system. He felt sure he had acquired the essential components required for a successful release as he got ready for his next trip. Still, one important point he had not quite appreciated—the use of analytics.

Opsy's next offering was a thorough webinar series covering cutting-edge digital marketing strategies. The possible influence of the show thrilled him, hence he put great effort into producing excellent content and interesting advertising materials. He did, however, ignore the need of meticulously examining and evaluating facts to hone his plan and raise his outcomes.

Opsy chose to phone Maria to go over his plans as the launch day drew near. Maria, this webinar series greatly excites me. It will be really popular, in my opinion. I have concentrated on producing outstanding material and interesting marketing tools.

Maria answered politely but curiously. "That sounds wonderful, Opsy. Have you set up analytics to monitor your performance and compile data? Making data-driven judgments by means of data monitoring helps one to grasp what is working and what is not.

Opsy paused. "I haven't done much more than set up basic sales and sign-up tracking. Is it essential, in your opinion?

Maria spoke in a forceful voice. "Exactly. Analytics can reveal opportunities for development, the success of your marketing initiatives, and the behavior of your audience. Set up thorough tracking and routinely go over the data.

Driven to maximize his launch, Opsy chose to follow Maria's counsel. Using technologies like Google Analytics, Hotjar, and tracking capabilities of his email marketing platform, he configured thorough analytics. Dashboards he designed tracked important benchmarks such email open rates, website traffic, conversion rates, and engagement levels.

To find the most successful messaging and design aspects, Opsy also chose to run A/B testing for his email campaigns and landing pages. Emphasizing the advantages of the forthcoming webinar series, he wrote an email to his members urging them to register.

" hello everyone,

It gives me great pleasure to introduce our forthcoming webinar series on cutting-edge digital marketing approaches! These seminars will offer thorough analysis and practical ideas to enable you to advance your marketing. Don't miss it; register today to guarantee your seat!

Best, Opsy Bee." much

Opsy closely watched the data and adjusted depending on his observations as the launch went forward. He changed his messaging as he observed that some email subjects had better open rates. He also optimized those landing pages with the best conversion rates.

One evening Opsy got a note from Brian, a subscriber. "Hi Opsy,

I wanted to thanks for the interesting webinars. The material is excellent; I value the practical advice. The registration process seemed flawless, and the follow-up emails arrived at just the right time and relevance. Maintain the fantastic work!

Excellent, Brian <„

Opsy came away feeling successful. Responding fast, he thanked Brian for his comments and expressed thanks for the help.

When Opsy considered the experience, she came to see the value of analytics. He had been able to maximize his marketing activities, increase involvement, and produce better outcomes by regularly tracking data and basing judgments on it. His acquired insights let him modify his approach and produce a more successful launch.

The outcome was obvious as the launch came to end. High attendance rates and favorable participant comments during the webinar series helped it to be successful. A big part of getting these results was Opsy's readiness to welcome analytics.

Ozzy knew the road was far from finished as he rejoiced with Maria and Jay. The story of the product introduction carried fresh difficulties and insights in every chapter. Equipped with the wisdom from his most recent launch, Opsy was prepared to face whatever happened next.

Epilogue: The Journey Continues

Surrounded by reminders of his journey—vision boards, notebooks full of ideas, and accolades from his successful product launches—Opsy Bee stood in his home office. When he considered the road he had chosen, he felt great fulfillment. Along with many obstacles, he had gained priceless knowledge and developed personally as a digital marketer and entrepreneur.

Osy's path had been everything from seamless. He had made blunders, suffered unanticipated losses, and had to react fast to shifting conditions. Still, every difficulty had taught him something fresh, which helped him to become the strong and informed marketer he is now.

Looking back, Opsy came to see that the value of tenacity was the most important thing he had discovered. Success was about learning from mistakes and keeping on, no matter how challenging the road seemed—not about avoiding them.

Opsy decided one evening to share his ideas with Maria and Jay by phone. Maria, Jay, then I wanted to thank you both for your direction and support over this road. I could not have learnt so much without you. It has been really enlightening.

Maria spoke with great pride. "Opsy, seeing how much you have grown has been amazing. You have come out stronger having squarely addressed every obstacle. Remember; the road does not stop here; fresh chances and lessons to learn will constantly present themselves.

Jay's reply was likewise upbeat. "Opsy, I'm happy of how far you've come and you've accomplished so much. Keep ahead, be inquisitive, and keep facing every obstacle. The future is bright, and it excites me to find out what it holds for you.

Inspired, Opsy chose to chronicle his path and the knowledge he had gained in a brand-new book. He wanted to impart his knowledge and advice to other budding digital marketers so they might negotiate their own roadways.

Opsy poured his heart and soul into the book as he wrote for the next several months. He related his successes and setbacks, his missteps, and the priceless knowledge he had gained. The cathartic approach let him consider his development and confirm his knowledge of the requirements for success in the realm of digital marketing.

Opsy felt quite successful when the book was at last finished. He called it "Adventures of a Guru-Wannabe: The Product Launch Saga," catching the core of his path and the continuous character of his search for achievement and knowledge.

Opsy emailed his readers to let them know his new book would be out and to offer some thoughts.

"Hi everyone,

It gives me great pleasure to share the publication of my new book, "Adventures of a Guru-Wannabe: The Product Launch Saga." This book is a mirror of my path, full of lessons discovered and obstacles confronted. For your personal road, I hope it offers insightful analysis and motivation.

We value your ongoing support. The road ahead excites me to see where it leads.

Good, Osy Bee"His crowd responded with an almost perfect rating. Many members expressed their enthusiasm and thanks, noting how much Opsy's experiences had taught them and how his story had motivated them to follow their own aspirations.

One email particularly noteworthy came from a subscriber called Emily. Hello Opsy,

We appreciate you bringing your trip forward for us. Your book is remarkably perceptive and motivating. It's comforting to see that mistakes and difficulties abound even among great marketers. Your narrative has given me the assurance to keep on my own road of discovery. Continue the great effort.

Ideally, Emily's

Opsy was filled with fresh direction and gratification. Reacting fast, he thanked Emily for her support and that he loved her gentle comments.

Opsy realized his road was far from finished as he gazed ahead. New challenges to overcome, fresh lessons to pick up, and fresh chances to grab would always present themselves. Equipped with his expertise and experience, Opsy was prepared to approach whatever lay ahead with resiliency and confidence.

Knowing that every difficulty presented a chance for development and every success evidence of his tenacity and dedication, Opsy Bee was resolved to welcome every stage of the product lsaunch story.

Milton Keynes UK
Ingram Content Group UK Ltd.
UKHW031831010924
447661UK00001B/89